“ HER NAME IS FARA ”

“ THAT DAYS THAT CHANGED EVERYTHING ”

ZUHAAN MANZOOR

Made with ♥ on the Notion Press Platform
www.notionpress.com

To Fara,

You are an exceptional girl with a maturity level beyond your years and a clear vision for everything. Your journey, from living up to the expectations of your family and society to chasing your dreams and ambitions, has been nothing short of inspiring.

Your relationship with Zuhaan, though brief, was intense and left a lasting impact on you. Your differing approaches to life and priorities ultimately led to your separation, but your strength and resilience in the face of that pain are truly remarkable.

Your story is a testament to the power of determination and the human spirit's ability to overcome adversity. May your experiences inspire others to believe in themselves and their ability to create their path in life.

With admiration and respect, [Zuhaan]

Contents

Foreword

Foreword:

Fara's story is one of love, resilience, and self-discovery. In this book, we follow Fara's journey as she navigates the challenges of growing up in a society that expects her to conform to traditional norms and values.

Despite her young age, Fara possesses a maturity level that goes beyond her years. She has a clear vision of what she wants in life and is determined to make a mark for herself. However, Fara's journey is not an easy one. She struggles with anger issues and anxiety, which makes her life all the more challenging.

The turning point in Fara's life comes when she meets Zuhaan, a gentle and kind-hearted boy who immediately strikes a chord with her. Their brief but intense relationship is filled with mutual affection and admiration, but ultimately their differences in priorities and thinking create a rift between them.

Fara's story is a reminder that love alone cannot overcome fundamental differences. It takes understanding, compromise, and a willingness to let go when necessary to move forward. Fara's journey of self-discovery and resilience is an inspiration to all of us to pursue our dreams and goals with determination and courage.

In this book, we witness Fara's journey of growth, her struggles with societal expectations, her relationships, and her ultimate realization that she deserves better. Fara's story is a testament to the strength of the human spirit and the power of determination. I hope that readers will find inspiration and wisdom in Fara's story and that her journey will resonate with them as it has with me.

Preface

Preface:

This book tells the story of Fara, an exceptional young woman who lived in Tangpora Bypass Srinagar. Despite her youth, Fara possessed a level of maturity and clarity of vision beyond her years. However, she also had serious anger issues and suffered from anxiety, which made her life challenging.

Coming from a well-reputed family, Fara's life was never easy. She had to live up to the expectations of her family and society, which often left her feeling suffocated. But she was determined to make a mark for herself and carve out her own path.

This book chronicles Fara's journey, from her struggles to her successes. Along the way, she meets Zuhaan, a kind and gentle young man who immediately strikes a chord with her. Their conversations become an integral part of their daily lives, and Fara finds solace in Zuhaan's company.

However, despite their mutual affection, Fara and Zuhaan's relationship doesn't work out due to their fundamentally different approaches to life. Fara is a rebel who wants to break free from societal shackles and live life on her own terms, while Zuhaan is more traditional and believes in following societal norms. Their different priorities create a rift between them, which ultimately leads to their breakup.

Fara's story is a testament to the resilience of the human spirit and the power of determination. It reminds us that no matter how tough life gets, we have the strength within us to overcome it and emerge victorious. This book is a tale of love, heartbreak, self-discovery, and growth, and I hope it resonates with readers and inspires them to overcome their own challenges.

Acknowledgements

Acknowledgment:

Writing a book is never an easy task. It takes a lot of time, effort, and dedication to bring an idea to life. This book, "Her Name is Fara," would not have been possible without the support and encouragement of many people.

First and foremost, I would like to thank Fara for inspiring me to write this book. Their story is a testament to the resilience of the human spirit and the power of determination, and I am grateful for the opportunity to share it with others.

I would like to express my sincere gratitude to my family and friends for their unwavering support and encouragement throughout this journey. Your love and belief in me have kept me motivated and inspired to keep writing.

I am also indebted to my editor and publisher for their guidance and expertise. Your keen eye for detail and passion for storytelling have helped me shape this book into its final form.

Lastly, I want to thank the readers for giving this book a chance. I hope that Fara and Zuhaan's story will resonate with you and inspire you to never give up on your dreams .

Thank you all for being a part of this journey.

Sincerely, [Zuhaan]

Prologue

The wind was howling, and the sky was dark and ominous as Fara stood on the rooftop of her house, gazing out at the city below. The air was thick with tension, and Fara's heart was beating so loudly that she could hear it in her ears. She felt suffocated, trapped in a world that she didn't belong to.

Fara was just eighteen, but she had already seen more than her fair share of struggles. She came from a well-reputed family in Tangpora Bypass Srinagar, and with that came a set of expectations that she could never seem to meet. Fara was different, a rebel who wanted to break free from the shackles of society and live life on her own terms.

Despite her intelligence and wit, Fara's life was challenging. She had serious anger issues and was also suffering from some kind of anxiety, which only made things harder. But Fara was determined to make a mark for herself, to carve out her path, and follow her dreams.

One day, a boy named Zuhaan found Fara's contact number and decided to reach out to her. They started talking, and soon their conversations became an integral part of their daily routine. Fara found solace in Zuhaan's company, and Zuhaan appreciated Fara's intelligence and wit.

However, despite their mutual affection, Fara and Zuhaan's relationship never worked out because of their opposite thinking. Their different approaches to life created a rift between them, which ultimately led to their breakup.

Fara went on to focus on her own goals and ambitions, but she couldn't ignore the feelings of neglect and loneliness that had been building up inside her. She knew that it was time to move on. It wasn't the happy ending that she had hoped for, but it was a valuable lesson in love and the importance of understanding and compromise.

This is the story of Fara, a young woman who fought against all odds to live life on her own terms. It is a story of resilience, determination, and the power of the human spirit. It is a story that reminds us that no matter how tough life gets, we have the strength within us to overcome it and emerge victorious.

CHAPTER ONE

THAT 10 DAYS THAT CHANGED EVERYTHING;

Fara was an exceptional girl woman who lived in Tangpora Bypass Srinagar. Despite her young age of eighteen, she possessed a maturity level beyond her years and a clear vision for everything. However, Fara had serious anger issues and was also suffering from some kind of anxiety, which made her life challenging.

Coming from a well-reputed family, Fara's life was never easy. She had to live up to the expectations of her family and society, which often left her feeling suffocated. However, Fara was determined to make a mark for herself and carve out her path.

One day, a boy named Zuhaan found Fara's contact number and decided to reach out to her. Zuhaan was a gentle and kind-hearted person who immediately struck a chord with Fara. They started talking, and soon their conversations became an integral part of their daily routine.

Fara found solace in Zuhaan's company, and Zuhaan appreciated Fara's intelligence and wit. However, despite their mutual affection, Fara and Zuhaan's relationship never worked out because of their opposite thinking.

Fara was a rebel who wanted to break free from the shackles of society and live life on her own terms. Zuhaan, on the other hand, was more traditional and believed in following the norms set by society. Their different approaches to life created a rift between them, which ultimately led to their breakup.

Fara and Zuhaan wanted to stay together, but their love was not enough to overcome their fundamental differences. They had to move on and live their lives separately, with the memories of their brief but intense relationship forever etched in their minds.

Despite the pain of separation, Fara continued to follow her dreams and chase her ambitions. She knew that life was too short to waste on regret and what-ifs, and she was determined to make the most of it.

Fara's journey was not an easy one, but she emerged stronger and wiser from her experiences. Her clear vision and maturity helped her navigate through the ups and downs of life, and her anger issues and anxiety gradually became manageable.

Fara's story is a testament to the resilience of the human spirit and the power of determination. It reminds us that no matter how tough life gets, we have the strength within us to overcome it and emerge victorious.

As time passed, Fara's understanding of Zuhaan's priorities began to clash with her own desires. While she admired Zuhaan's ambition, she couldn't shake the feeling that their relationship was being put on hold.

Fara started to feel lonely and neglected, and she couldn't help but wonder if Zuhaan was really the right person for her. She tried to communicate her feelings to Zuhaan, but he seemed unable to understand her perspective.

Their differences in priorities only seemed to widen the gap between them. Fara longed for the kind of attention and affection that she felt Zuhaan was unable to give, while Zuhaan felt frustrated that Fara couldn't appreciate the importance of his career.

Despite their love for each other, their relationship began to falter. They would argue and disagree, unable to find a compromise that worked for both of them. Fara felt that Zuhaan was holding her back, while Zuhaan felt that Fara was being unrealistic.

In the end, Fara realized that she couldn't force Zuhaan to change his priorities and that it was unfair to expect him to do so. She came to accept that they were simply not compatible and that they needed to part ways.

It was a difficult decision for Fara, but she knew that it was the right one. She couldn't ignore the feelings of neglect and loneliness that had been building up inside her, and she knew that she deserved better.

Fara went on to focus on her own goals and ambitions, and while she still thought of Zuhaan from time to time, she knew that it was time to move on. It wasn't the happy ending that she had hoped for, but it was a valuable lesson in love and the importance of understanding and compromise.

Zuhaan realized that he had found the right girl in Fara. She was intelligent, caring, and had a clear vision for her future. However, he also realized that he was not giving her what she deserved.

He was so focused on his career goals that he neglected the most important person in his life. Fara deserved his attention and care, but he had failed to give her that.

Fara, on the other hand, began to feel confused and unfulfilled in the relationship. She didn't feel the peace that she had expected to feel with Zuhaan. She wondered if she had made a mistake in choosing him as her partner.

As they continued to struggle with their differences, Fara began to realize that their relationship was not sustainable without mutual effort and compromise. She longed for a deeper connection and emotional intimacy that she felt Zuhaan was not capable of giving.

Despite her love for Zuhaan, Fara realized that it was time to move on. She knew that she deserved someone who would give her the attention and care she needed, and she couldn't wait for Zuhaan to change.

It was a difficult decision, but Fara knew it was the right one. She wished Zuhaan all the best in his career and life, but she knew that she needed to focus on her own happiness and well-being.

In the end, Fara found the strength to let go of a relationship that wasn't working for her. She learned that sometimes, despite our best efforts, some relationships are not meant to be. And that's okay. The important thing is to learn from our experiences and move forward with grace and resilience.

Despite their differences, Fara and Zuhaan were deeply in love. They had moments of intense connection and shared dreams for their future together. However, they also struggled with their egos and their stubbornness.

There were times when they would stop talking for days, each waiting for the other to make the first move. Fara would try to make Zuhaan understand how things actually worked, but he was practical and often saw things in a different light. He would try to do what she wanted, but his own desires and ambitions would often get in the way.

Their strong egos and tempers would often lead to arguments and hurt feelings. They both wanted to be right, and neither was willing to back down. But despite it all, they never stopped loving each other.

It took time and effort, but they eventually learned to communicate better and understand each other's perspectives. They found a way to work through their differences and support each other in their individual goals.

Fara learned to be patient with Zuhaan's practicality and to appreciate his efforts, even if they didn't always align with her own desires. Zuhaan, in turn, learned to listen more and to be more open to Fara's vision for their future.

Their love for each other was strong enough to overcome their ego and anger issues. They learned to compromise and find a balance that worked for both of them. In the end, their love and commitment to each other were stronger than anything that could come between them.

As Zuhaan picked up Fara and her friend Sana from LD road, there was noticeable tension in the car. The ride to Fat Panday was filled with silence, with no conversation between them. Fara and Zuhaan were lost in their own thoughts, and Sana was trying to ease the tension by making small talk.

After they arrived at the restaurant, they ordered their food and sat quietly, each lost in their own thoughts. Zuhaan couldn't help but feel that their relationship was just not working out. He wanted to make it work, but he felt that Fara's expectations were too high.

Fara, on the other hand, was feeling frustrated and hurt. She had been waiting for Zuhaan to make an effort, and even though he had taken the time to meet her, it didn't feel like enough. She wanted him to understand her and support her dreams, but it seemed like they were always at odds with each other.

As the night wore on, they finished their meal and left the restaurant, still lost in their own thoughts. The ride back to LD road was just as quiet as before. Zuhaan dropped them off and said a polite goodbye, but Fara knew that their relationship was in trouble.

As she walked into her house, she couldn't help but feel a sense of sadness and disappointment. She had hoped that things would work out between them, but it seemed like their differences were too great to overcome. Fara knew that she needed to take some time to think about what she really wanted and whether Zuhaan was the right person for her

Fara and Zuhaan had been in a relationship for over a year, but lately, things were not going well. They were constantly arguing and disagreeing on everything. Fara could feel the distance between them growing, but she couldn't understand why Zuhaan was not leaving her.

Despite their troubles, they both clung to the relationship, unwilling to let go. Fara couldn't bear the thought of being without Zuhaan, and Zuhaan couldn't imagine his life without Fara. They continued to hold on, even though they both knew that something wasn't right.

One day, Zuhaan finally realized that he was wasting his time as well as Fara's. He knew that they were complete opposites and that they had very little in common. He couldn't understand why they had even started dating in the first place.

Zuhaan decided that it was time to end things between them. He didn't want to continue living in a relationship that wasn't making him happy. He knew that it was going to be difficult, but he had to be honest with himself and with Fara.

When Zuhaan broke the news to Fara, she was devastated. She couldn't believe that their relationship was over, and she didn't understand why Zuhaan was giving up on them. Fara begged Zuhaan to reconsider, but he was firm in his decision.

Although it was painful, Fara eventually realized that Zuhaan was right. They were not meant to be together, and it was time to move on. They parted ways, but Fara knew that it was for the best. She would always cherish the memories they shared, but it was time to let go and find happiness elsewhere.

In the days following their breakup, Fara struggled to come to terms with the end of her relationship with Zuhaan. She found herself constantly thinking about him and wondering what could have been different. She missed him terribly, but at the same time, she knew that it was time to let go and move on.

Fara threw herself into her work and her hobbies, hoping to distract herself from the pain. She spent more time with her friends and family, and slowly but surely, she began to feel better. She realized that there was more to life than just being in a relationship.

Meanwhile, Zuhaan was also struggling with the aftermath of their breakup. He missed Fara and regretted hurting her, but he knew that it was the right decision.

After their breakup, Zuhaan and Fara tried to maintain some level of contact, but it was clear that things were not the same between them. Zuhaan struggled with the decision he had made, but he knew that it was for the best. He still cared deeply for Fara and wanted the best for her.

One day, Zuhaan called Fara to talk. He told her that he had been thinking a lot about their relationship and the decision he had made to end things. He explained that he didn't want to be apart from her, but it seemed like destiny had other plans.

Fara listened carefully to what Zuhaan had to say, and although she was still hurt by the breakup, she understood where he was coming from. She knew that sometimes things just don't work out, no matter how much two people may care for each other.

Zuhaan went on to express his admiration for Fara's cool, understanding nature. He told her that anyone who is lucky enough to have her in their life will be truly fortunate. He praised her intelligence, maturity, and open-mindedness, saying that he hoped she would continue to achieve great things and make her parents proud.

Fara was touched by Zuhaan's words, and it gave her a new perspective on their relationship. She realized that sometimes, even though things may not work out between two people, there can still be a sense of respect and admiration for one another.

From that day forward, Zuhaan and Fara remained on good terms. They continued to have mutual respect for each other, and they both moved on with their lives. Although their romantic relationship was over, they knew that they would always have a special place in each other's hearts.

After their breakup, Zuhaan and Fara tried to maintain some level of contact, but it was clear that things were not the same between them. Zuhaan struggled with the decision he had made, but he knew that it was for the best. He still cared deeply for Fara and wanted the best for her.

One day, Zuhaan called Fara to talk. He told her that he had been thinking a lot about their relationship and the decision he had made to end things. He explained that he didn't want to be apart from her, but it seemed like destiny had other plans.

Fara listened carefully to what Zuhaan had to say, and although she was still hurt by the breakup, she understood where he was coming from. She knew that sometimes things just don't work out, no matter how much two people may care for each other.

Zuhaan went on to express his admiration for Fara's cool, understanding nature. He told her that anyone who is lucky enough to have her in their life will be truly fortunate. He praised her intelligence, maturity, and open-mindedness, saying that he hoped she would continue to achieve great things and make her parents proud.

Fara was touched by Zuhaan's words, and it gave her a new perspective on their relationship. She realized that sometimes, even though things may not work out between two people, there can still be a sense of respect and admiration for one another.

From that day forward, Zuhaan and Fara remained on good terms. They continued to have mutual respect for each other, and they both moved on with their lives. Although their romantic relationship was over, they knew that they would always have a special place in each other's hearts.

As Zuhaan sat alone with his thoughts, he couldn't help but feel a sense of pride when he thought about Fara. Despite the fact that their romantic relationship had come to an end, he still cared deeply for her and wanted the best for her.

"I wish Fara all the success in the world," he thought to himself. "I hope she reaches the heights of the sky, and that her parents are proud of the daughter they raised. I'm proud of her too, even if things didn't work out between us."

Zuhaan knew that Fara was capable of achieving great things. She was smart, driven, and had a passion for helping others. He had always admired her for her dedication to her studies and her desire to make a positive impact on the world.

"I know that Fara has what it takes to make a difference," Zuhaan thought to himself. "She's not afraid to stand up for what she believes in, and she's always willing to put in the hard work to achieve her goals."

Even though he couldn't be with her anymore, he knew that he would always support her from afar. He hoped that she would continue to follow her dreams and that she would find happiness and success in all of her future endeavors.

"I just want her to know that I believe in her," Zuhaan thought. "Even though we're not together anymore, I'll always be rooting for her."

"On 23rd February 2023, we ended our journey together," Zuhaan thought to himself. "It's time for me to break all contact with her. If I don't, I'll only suffer more. But even though we won't be in touch, I still want to see her one last time."

Zuhaan knew that he couldn't leave things unsaid. He needed to tell Fara how he felt, even if it was just once more. So, he secretly arranged to meet her at a coffee shop, where they used to hang out during happier times.

When Fara arrived, Zuhaan's heart skipped a beat. She looked as beautiful as ever, and he couldn't help feeling a sense of sadness at the thought of never seeing her again.

"Hey Fara," he said softly. "I just wanted to tell you that no matter how our journey ends, I will miss you. I still have so much respect for you, and I've learned a lot of valuable lessons from you. Thank you for being a part of my life."

Fara's eyes welled up with tears as she listened to Zuhaan's words. She had never doubted his love for her, but hearing him say these things one last time made her heartache.

"I'll miss you too, Zuhaan," Fara whispered. "I'll always treasure the memories we made together."

After that, the two of them sat in silence, each lost in their own thoughts. When it was time to leave, they hugged each other tightly, knowing that it was the last time they would ever see each other.

As Zuhaan walked away, he couldn't help feeling a sense of sadness, but also a sense of closure. He knew that it was time for them to move on, but he would always treasure the memories of the time they spent together.

The End of Fara and Zuhaan's Relationship

It was a typical Tuesday evening when Zuhaan and Fara's relationship came to an end. Zuhaan had just come back from work, and he was looking forward to spending some quality time with Fara. But when he entered their apartment, he found Fara in tears.

"What's wrong, Fara?" Zuhaan asked concern etched on his face.

Fara looked up at him with red, puffy eyes. "I miss him," she said, her voice barely above a whisper.

Zuhaan's heart sank as he realized who Fara was talking about. Fahad, her ex-boyfriend, had left her heartbroken and shattered just a few months ago. Zuhaan had been there for Fara, listening to her cries and soothing her pain. He had hoped that with time, Fara would be able to move on and leave Fahad in the past. But now it seemed like that was not the case.

"Fara, we need to talk," Zuhaan said, trying to sound calm.

Fara looked at him, her eyes pleading with him to understand. "I can't help it, Zuhaan. I can't just turn off my feelings for Fahad. I love him, but I don't want him back. I just miss him so much."

Zuhaan took a deep breath, trying to steady himself. He knew what he had to do, but it didn't make it any easier.

"Fara, I can't be with someone who still has feelings for their ex. I care about you, but I can't compete with someone who is not even here," Zuhaan said, his voice firm but gentle.

Fara's eyes widened in shock as she realized what Zuhaan was saying. "Are you breaking up with me?" she asked, her voice trembling.

Zuhaan nodded his heart heavy with sadness. "I think it's for the best, Fara. I want you to be happy, but I can't be the one who makes you forget about Fahad. You need to do that on your own."

Fara nodded slowly, the tears still streaming down her face. "I understand," she said, her voice barely above a whisper.

And with those words, Fara and Zuhaan's relationship came to an end. Zuhaan left the apartment, leaving Fara alone to face her feelings and come to terms with what had just happened. As he walked out, he looked back at Fara one last time, wishing things could have been different. But sometimes, love is not enough to overcome the pain of the past, and we have to let go in order to move forward.

Zuhaan sat on his bed, his phone pressed to his ear as he listened to Fara's sobs on the other end of the line. He had called her to check up on her, as they still maintained a friendship despite their breakup. He had no idea what he was in for.

"Zuhaan, I just can't take it anymore," Fara sobbed. "I've been carrying this burden in my heart for so long, and I can't keep it inside anymore."

Zuhaan's heart ached as he listened to her cry. He had always known Fara to be a soft-hearted and emotional person, but this was different. Her sobs were deep and guttural as if she was releasing years of pent-up emotions.

"Fara, what's going on? What's wrong?" Zuhaan asked, trying to keep his own voice steady.

"Fahad," Fara choked out between sobs. "I can't unlove him, Zuhaan. I can't erase him from my heart, but I don't want him back either. It's just so hard."

Zuhaan's heart sank. He knew that Fara had been in a serious relationship with Fahad before they got together, but he had assumed that Fara had moved on. He didn't know that she was still carrying the weight of her past relationship.

"Fara, I had no idea," Zuhaan said softly. "I'm here for you. You can talk to me about anything."

And Fara did. She poured out her heart to Zuhaan, telling him about her struggles to let go of Fahad and move on with her life. She spoke about her fears of being alone and her anxieties about the future. Zuhaan listened patiently, his heart breaking for her.

After what felt like hours, Fara's sobs finally subsided, and she took a deep breath.

"Thank you, Zuhaan," she said softly. "I feel like a weight has been lifted off my shoulders. I'm sorry for burdening you with all of this."

"Hey, don't apologize," Zuhaan said firmly. "You're not a burden. I care about you, Fara, and I always will. We may not be together romantically anymore, but that doesn't mean I don't still care about you."

Fara was silent for a moment before she spoke again.

"I'm lucky to have you as a friend, Zuhaan," she said. "Thank you for being there for me."

Zuhaan smiled, feeling a warmth spread through his chest. He may not have been able to fix Fara's heartache, but he could be there for her as a friend. And that was enough.

"You're welcome, Fara," he said. "Anytime."

Zuhaan sat with a heavy heart as he recounted the story of Fara's late boyfriend, Burhan. He took a deep breath before starting, knowing how much this topic affected Fara.

"Fara used to talk a lot about Burhan," Zuhaan said, his voice soft and thoughtful. "They were together for four years, and she loved him deeply. But then he was diagnosed with cancer, and everything changed."

Zuhaan could see the pain etched on Fara's face as she talked about Burhan. He remembered how she would cry herself to sleep, and how she would often shut herself away from the world for days at a time.

"It was hard for her to watch Burhan suffer like that," Zuhaan continued. "And when he passed away, it was like a part of her died too. She carried that burden with her for a long time, and it killed her inside."

Zuhaan paused for a moment, lost in thought. He knew that Fara was still grieving, even after all these years. It was something that never truly went away.

"But Fara is a fighter," Zuhaan said, his voice filled with conviction. "She may have been broken, but she didn't let it destroy her. She picked herself up and kept going, even when it felt impossible. And that's what makes her so strong."

As Zuhaan finished speaking, he could see the sadness in his friends' eyes. He knew that Fara's pain was something that affected them all, but he hoped that by sharing her story, they could understand her better.

"Fara may carry that burden with her always, but she's also a survivor," Zuhaan said, a small smile playing on his lips. "And I know that she will continue to fight, no matter what life throws at her."

Dear Fara,

As I write this message, my heart is filled with a sense of sadness and longing. Our time together may have been brief, but it was intense and meaningful, and I will always cherish the memories we shared.

I want you to know that I understand the pain and burden you carry in your heart. Losing someone you love is never easy, and I can only imagine how difficult it must have been for you to cope with Burhan's death. But I also want you to know that you are not alone. I am here for you, even if we can't be together as a couple.

You are a strong and resilient person, Fara, and I have always admired your determination and clear vision for your life. I know that you will find a way to overcome your pain and continue to pursue your dreams. And if you ever need someone to talk to or a shoulder to cry on, I am here for you.

Please take care of yourself, Fara, and know that you will always hold a special place in my heart.

With love and admiration,

" Zuhaan "

Printed by Libri Plureos GmbH in Hamburg,
Germany